BIBLE TRANSLATION DIFFERENCES

Criteria for Excellence in Reading and Choosing a Bible Translation

LELAND RYKEN

CROSSWAY BOOKS

A DIVISION OF
GOOD NEWS PUBLISHERS
WHEATON, ILLINOIS

Library of Congress Cataloging-in-Publication Data
Ryken, Leland.
   Bible translation differences : criteria for excellence in reading and choosing a Bible translation / Leland Ryken.
     p. cm.
   Includes bibliographical references.
   ISBN 1-58134-643-3 (tpb)
   1. Bible—Translating I. Title.
BS449.R948   2004
220.5'2—dc22   2004012676

CH		14	13	12	11	10	09	08	07	06	05	04
15	14	13	12	11	10	9	8	7	6	5	4	3	2	1

CONTENTS

1

How Do Bible Translations Differ from Each Other?

I WANT TO BEGIN BY surveying and critiquing what has been happening in Bible translation for the past fifty years. If I am right, few laypeople know what *really* makes various English Bible translations different from each other (see Appendix: Bible Translations Chart). When one of my colleagues in the Bible Department at Wheaton College polls his students about Bible translations, he finds that they begin with the premise that all modern translations are equally accurate as renditions of the original text, and that the only basis for preferring one over another is the criterion of readability. In my judgment, this is a matter for serious concern.

But who am I to sit in judgment on this state of unawareness? When I joined the Translation Oversight Committee of the English Standard Version of the Bible, at our first meeting the president of the publishing company announced that the ESV would be an essentially literal translation. I had no idea what that meant, nor how an essentially literal translation differs from its implied alternative. Since that moment of embarrassing ignorance, I *have* learned what the issues are, and I have become alarmed at what happened to Bible translation about four decades ago. So let me attempt a brief history and analysis of where we stand in English Bible translation.

1. The Goal of Bible Translation

Until the middle of the twentieth century, English Bible translation was governed by the assumption that the goal of Bible translation was to translate the words of the original Hebrew and Greek texts insofar as the process of translation allows. I know of no major, widely used English Bible before the middle of the twentieth century that did not primarily aim to reproduce in English the words of the original. William Tyndale, from whom English Bible translation largely flows, even coined words like *intercession* and *atonement* so as to be faithful to the actual words of the Greek text. Alister McGrath, in his book on the King James Version, claims that a careful study of the way in which the King James Bible translates the Greek and Hebrew originals shows that the translators tried (a) to ensure that every word in the original had an English equivalent, (b) to highlight all words added to the original for the sake of intelligibility, and (c) to follow the word order of the original where possible.[1]

Around the middle of the twentieth century, a theory of translation known as dynamic equivalence became the fashionable translation theory. Dynamic equivalence, more recently sailing under the name functional equivalence, has as its aim to reproduce not the words of the original text but the ideas or thoughts. The impetus for this theory came from translators who were translating the Bible into new languages on the mission field. The influential scholars behind the movement were Kenneth Pike and Eugene Nida.

It was simply assumed that what was considered best for the mission field would also be best for English Bible translation. This is very significant, and it was in my view a serious mistake. I say that because the English Bible had through the centuries become so familiar and well-established that it should have never been put into the same category as a Bible being translated into a language that had just been reduced to an alphabet.

2. THOUGHT-FOR-THOUGHT OR WORD-FOR-WORD?

How should we define dynamic equivalence? Dynamic equivalence is a theory of translation based on the premise that whenever something in the original text is foreign or unclear to a contemporary English reader, the original text should be translated in terms of an equivalent rather than literally. In actual practice, dynamic equivalence goes far beyond this by frequently making interpretive decisions for the reader and adding commentary to the text. Dynamic equivalence is popularly known as a thought-for-thought translation instead of a word-for-word translation.

Many readers do not realize the far-reaching significance of what is being said by means of specialized language in the prefaces to dynamic equivalent translations. Here are some representative quotations (with italics added to highlight the key phrases):

- "[The translator's] first task was to understand correctly *the meaning* of the original" (GNB).
- ". . . a *thought-for-thought* translation" (NLT).
- ". . . to reclothe *the meaning* of the original in the words and structure of American English" (SEB).
- "The first concern of the translators has been . . . fidelity to *the thought* of the biblical writers" (NIV).

It is easy to miss what is being *denied* in these statements. What is being denied is that the translator has any responsibility to translate the exact *words* of the original. I am not saying that dynamic equivalent translators pay no attention to the words of the original. I am saying that they feel no obligation to express the exact words of the original in English. By contrast, essentially literal translations *do* strive to retain the words of the original, as they make clear in their prefaces.[2]

Here is my concern: Most readers of dynamic equivalent translations do not have any understanding as to the liberties that have been taken with the words of the original text. What dynamic translators give us is a translation plus a commentary, but we have no way of knowing where translation ends and the translation committee's commentary begins.

The most revealing thing that I uncovered while doing the research for my book was what I found in the prefaces to dynamic equivalent translations. As you read the following sample statements, I invite you to see if you can catch the common thread (italics have been added to highlight the key phrases):

- This translation seeks "to express the meaning in a manner and form easily understood by *the readers*" (GNB).
- "Metaphorical language is often difficult *for contemporary readers* to understand, so at times we have chosen to translate or illuminate the metaphor" (NLT).
- "Because *for most readers* today the phrases 'the Lord of hosts' and 'God of hosts' have little meaning, this version renders them 'the Lord Almighty' and 'God Almighty'" (NIV).
- "Ancient customs are often unfamiliar *to modern readers*" (NEW CENTURY VERSION).
- "We have used the vocabulary and language structures . . . *of a junior high student*" (NLT).

Who is calling the shots for these translations—the biblical author or the modern reader? As John MacArthur has noted, such translations "diminish the glory of divine revelation by being more concerned with the human reader than the divine author." It is very revealing what Eugene Nida, the founder of dynamic equivalence, said in an interview that *Christianity Today* carried.[3] Nida made no attempt to conceal his scorn for translators who think that the original words themselves need to be translated. He said that these people are guilty of "word worship," that "they don't understand the text," and that "they worship words instead of worshiping God as revealed in Jesus Christ."

During the last half century the proponents of dynamic equivalence have dominated Bible translation and have become increasingly bold in disparaging advocates of essentially literal translation. Nearly all new modern Bible translations before the English Standard Version have been dynamic equivalent translations.[4] As biblical scholar Ray Van Leeuwen said in an article entitled "We Really Do Need Another Bible Translation," "If you [have] read a Bible translated in the last half-century, you [have] probably read a Bible influenced by Nida."[5]

2

FIVE NEGATIVE EFFECTS OF DYNAMIC EQUIVALENCE

WHAT, IN MY VIEW, are the negative effects of dynamic equivalent translations? For our purposes here, I will mention five of these:

1. TAKING LIBERTIES IN TRANSLATION

First, dynamic equivalence takes liberties in translating the precise wording of the original that we would not allow in other areas of life. I entitled the second chapter of my book *The Word of God in English* "Lessons from Ordinary Discourse," and in it I surveyed some everyday situations to test whether we usually consider it important to have the exact wording of an author or speaker. Let me just mention a few categories without taking time to spell out the details. Here are everyday types of discourse where I think it matters a lot that we have the exact words of the source: love letters, marriage vows, legal documents, contracts, accident reports, a memorable statement from a sermon, memoirs of a grandmother, recipes, a compliment or criticism, a quote from an interview, instructions for assembling an appliance.

My conclusion after exploring these matters was that it is only in a minority of everyday situations that we think that only the thought or idea of what was said will suffice and that the precise wording is unimportant. You might stop to think about something that you have written, something that you regarded as a very important statement intended for an audience and that you labored over to make sure that it said exactly what you intended. Then stop to think how you would feel if an editor serving as an intermediary had done the following things with what you had written:

- changed words that were deemed old-fashioned or difficult into more contemporary and colloquial language;
- changed a metaphor to direct statement because of an assumption that your audience could not handle figurative language;
- changed a statement that the editor feared would not be immediately understandable to match what the editor believed that you intended with your statement;
- eliminated a word that the editor regarded as a technical theological term and replaced it with a plain, non-technical term;
- consistently turned your carefully crafted, longer sentences into short, choppy sentences because the editor assumed that your audience could not handle a sentence as long as what you had written;
- reduced the level of vocabulary to a seventh-grade level;
- changed your gender references to match the editor's ideas on gender language.

Would you object to all of this? I would object on the ground that we do not allow such liberties to be taken with what an author has written—certainly not without the original author's agreement and prior consent.

I trust that my list of changes is instantly recognizable as exactly the things that dynamic equivalent translators do and that some of them make explicit in their prefaces, or if not in their prefaces, then in the theoretic literature that lays out the rules for dynamic equivalence.

The resulting question for Bible translation runs something like this: Is it likely to be more important or less important to preserve the original wording of the Bible than it is with everyday discourse? Stated another way, if getting the exact wording is important in most kinds of everyday discourse, is it not important to strive for this as far as possible when we translate the Bible from the original into English?

Here is the crux of the matter: Dynamic equivalent translators have used the process of translation to do all sorts of things with the Bible that we would not tolerate being done with documents in their original language. The process of translation has been used as the occasion for license. Scholar D. A. Carson stigmatizes my position as "linguistic conservatism." I *endorse* linguistic conservatism, by which I mean a translation that seeks to convey the words of the original text as much as the translation process allows. The other translation theory strikes me as linguistic license.

2. DESTABILIZATION OF THE TEXT

This brings me to my second harm regarding dynamic equivalence. Dynamic equivalent translations have destabilized the biblical text by multiplying variant translations of many Bible passages. There are at least two reasons for this. First, it is a fact that scholars do not agree on the meanings of many Bible passages. All you need to do to confirm this is start reading around in Bible commentaries. Dynamic equivalent translators, however, import the variability in their interpretation of the Bible into their translation of the Bible.

Secondly, once we adopt the premise that it is only the thought of the Bible that needs to be translated, and not the words, then once a translation committee decides what a passage means, it is free to use whatever English words it wishes to express what it thinks the meaning of the passage is. There are no adequate controls on interpretation here. The control *should be* fidelity to the words of the original.

Let's look at some examples of this destabilizing of the text. Here is how three modern translations that belong to the "essentially literal" camp have translated the conclusion of John 6:27:

- ". . . for on Him the Father, *even* God, has set His seal" (NASB).
- ". . . because God the Father has set His seal on Him" (NKJV).
- "For on him God the Father has set his seal" (ESV).

These are slightly different, but the text is stable.

Now look at how dynamic equivalent translations have rendered the statement:

- "On him God the Father has placed his seal of approval" (NIV, TNIV).
- ". . . for on him God the Father has set the seal of his authority" (REB).
- ". . . because God the Father has given him the right to do so" (CEV).
- "For God the Father has sent me for that very purpose" (NLT).
- "He and what he does are guaranteed by God the Father to last" (*The Message*).

This is a destabilized text. The same Greek words are translated into English words that have widely divergent meanings. The result is that we lose confidence in the reliability of what the family of dynamic equivalent translations offer with this verse. How could we not lose confidence, when the meaning varies so widely? The variation is so great that, as I was compiling the list, I had to "double check" to make sure I had the right verse with some of the translations.

Dynamic equivalent translators believe that the translator has the duty to make interpretive decisions for the ignorant reader. Eugene Nida, for example, claims that "the average reader is usually much less capable of making correct judgments about . . . alternative meanings than is the translator, who can make use of the best scholarly judgments on ambiguous passages."[6] But if this is true, why is it that translators, with their allegedly superior and reliable knowledge, cannot agree among themselves? Instead of leading the Bible reading public into a better grasp of the original text, dynamic equivalent translations have confused the public by multiplying the range of renditions of various Bible passages.

If we ask why dynamic equivalent translations have destabilized the text, the answer is obvious: There are no adequate controls on the translation process. Once a translation committee does not feel bound to translate the words of the original but only the ideas, and once it decides to its satisfaction what a passage means, it is free then to choose whatever words it thinks best express the meaning that it has decided is correct. Clearly more controls on translation than this are needed.

As a footnote to what I have said thus far about the way in which dynamic equivalent translators openly say that they do not feel bound to express the exact words of the original, I want to mention in passing something called verbal or plenary inspiration of the Bible. This doctrine asserts not only that God inspired the *thoughts* of biblical writers, but that inspiration extends to their *words*. The impetus for restating this doctrine with vigor a century ago was the claims of liberal theology that only the general thought or ideas of the Bible are inspired, not the details. Numerous passages in the Bible, however, show the importance of the very words of the Bible. A good example is Jesus' response to Satan that "Man shall not live by bread alone, but by *every word* that comes from the mouth of God" (Matt. 4:4), or Jesus' statement that "the words that I have spoken to you are spirit and life" (John 6:63). (See also Exod. 19:6; Deut. 32:46-47; Prov. 30:5; John 17:8, 17; Luke 21:33; Rev. 21:5; Rev. 22:18-19.)

3. WHAT THE BIBLE "MEANS" VS. WHAT THE BIBLE SAYS

It is an easy step from my second main point—that dynamic equivalent translations lack adequate controls on translation—to my next point that dynamic equivalent translations often make it impossible to know what the Bible means because they remove from sight what the Bible says. In this regard, dynamic equivalent translation fails to deliver what most readers think that they are getting. What is the unstated assumption with which we read an English translation? That what we are reading is "what the Bible says." Surely as general readers this is how we would express it. But dynamic equivalent translations regularly do *not* give us what the Bible says. They give us the translation committee's preferred interpretation of what the text means. And since a dynamic equivalent translation is often a translation plus an interpretive commentary, we do not know where one ends and the other begins.

When dynamic equivalent translations remove what the original says from sight, they short-circuit the process of biblical interpretation. I recently heard an expository sermon on Psalm 24, the last verse of which reads, "Who is this King of glory? / The LORD of hosts, / he is the King of glory!"[7] Now in regard to the last verse of Psalm 24, the NIV does not preserve what the original says with the phrase "the Lord of hosts." In fact, the NIV preface singles out this phrase as one regarding which the translators decided that "because for most readers today the phrases 'the Lord of hosts' and 'God of hosts' have little meaning, this version renders them 'the Lord Almighty' and 'God Almighty.'" By removing the phrase "Lord of hosts" from sight, the NIV makes it impossible for a reader to see a legitimate reference to the armies or citizens of heaven—created beings who are under God's command in heaven. Furthermore, some commentators, my pastor among them, see in this last verse of Psalm 24 an eschatological level of meaning—in other words, a reference to the redeemed saints in the presence of God in heaven.

As scholar Ray Van Leeuwen says in his excellent writing on this subject, "It is hard to know what the Bible *means* when we are uncertain about what it *says*. . . . The problem with [functional equivalent] translations (i.e., most modern translations) is that they prevent the reader from inferring biblical *meaning* because they change what the Bible *said*."[8] To confirm this, we can compare translations of Psalm 23:5a. A literal translation is, "You anoint my head with oil." Compare that to three dynamic equivalent translations:

- "You welcome me as an honored guest" (GNB).
- "You welcome me as a guest, anointing my head with oil" (NLT).
- "You honor me as your guest" (CEV).

Are these good interpretations of the verse? How can you know if what the original says—"you anoint my head with oil"—has been removed from sight or mingled with other material?

Similarly, a common New Testament metaphor for the Christian life is a path down which one walks. For example, 1 Thessalonians 2:12 reads, "Walk in a manner worthy of God" (NASB, ESV; KJV, NKJV, "walk worthy of God"). Dynamic equivalent translations render the word *walk* by the abstraction *live* (NIV, NLT, REB, TNIV), and English readers have no way of knowing that they have been given a substitute.

What are the negative effects of dynamic equivalent translations? Thus far I have provided three answers: (1) dynamic equivalence makes changes in the original text that we do not allow even in the ordinary situations of life; (2) it lacks adequate controls on the translation process and as a result has destabilized the text of the English Bible; and (3) it regularly replaces what the Bible says with a translation committee's verdict on what the Bible means.

4. FALLING SHORT OF WHAT WE SHOULD EXPECT

My fourth objection against dynamic equivalent translations is that, because of what I have already said, these translations fall short of what the Bible reading public should rightfully expect. After all, what is the minimal assumption we make when we pick up any book, whether a Bible translation or novel? We assume that we have before us what the author actually wrote, subject to the necessary changes required by translation if the book is a translation. As a reader of the English Bible, I assume that the translation I am reading expresses what the Bible says. This is what I *want* in an English Bible translation. If I want commentary on what the text means, I can go to commentaries. But dynamic equivalent translations are actually hybrids. Dynamic equivalent translators add the functions of editor and exegete to the translator's job description.

What, then, do dynamic equivalent translators feel free to do?

Here is a list that can be readily confirmed from both prefaces to dynamic equivalent translations and the actual translations: Dynamic equivalent translators . . .

- reduce the level of vocabulary used by the original authors;

- drop figurative language and replace it with literal statements that represent the translator's preferred interpretation;
- change words that are considered either difficult or "not how *we* would say it";
- change what the original authors wrote to what the translators think they intended;
- change gender references to reflect current views on gender language;
- chop down the length of sentences to a series of shorter sentences.

Why do I claim that doing these kinds of things is misleading to the Bible reading public? For the simple reason that dynamic equivalent translations have not done everything possible to inform the public of the liberties that have been taken with the original text. And even if dynamic equivalent translations did explain these liberties in their prefaces, most Bible readers do not normally read and/or understand prefaces. Most readers operate on the legitimate premise that they have been given, subject to the necessary changes of translation, words that correspond to the words of the biblical authors.

Below is an example of what I am talking about. I have listed a range of how modern translations have rendered a key phrase in Romans 1:5. The question that I want you to ponder as you read through the list is how you can differentiate what the original actually says from interpretation by a translation committee. In each case, I have italicized the key phrase that we need to compare.

- "Through him I received the privilege of an apostolic commission to bring people of all nations *to faith and obedience* in his name" (REB and TNIV are identical on the key phrase).

- "Through him and for his name's sake, we received grace and apostleship to call people from among all the Gentiles *to the obedience that comes from faith*" (NIV).
- "Jesus was kind to me and chose me to be an apostle, so that people of all nations *would obey and have faith*" (CEV).
- "Through Christ, God has given us the privilege and authority to tell Gentiles everywhere what God has done for them, *so that they will believe and obey him*, bringing glory to his name" (NLT).
- ". . . through whom we have received grace and apostleship to bring about *the obedience of faith* for the sake of his name among all the nations" (ESV).

Which of these translations reproduces what the original actually says? To answer that, one would need to know Greek, someone will protest—which is exactly the point. But the reader of an English translation *should* be able to have confidence that a translation has not tampered with the original.

Only the last translation in the list reproduces the phrase "the obedience of faith" as it appears in the original text. The other translations have added an interpretive slant to this phrase, and we should note that they do not agree among themselves as to what the correct interpretation is.

5. A Logical and Linguistic Impossibility

A final objection that I wish to raise against dynamic equivalence is that it is based on a logical and linguistic impossibility. Dynamic equivalence claims to translate the thought *rather than* the words of the original. My claim is that this is impossible. The fallacy of thinking that a translation should translate the meaning rather than the words of the original is simple: There is no such a thing as disembodied thought, emancipated from words. Ideas and thoughts depend on words and are expressed by them.

When we change the words, we change the meaning. An expert on Bible translation has expressed the matter thus:

> Language is not a mere receptacle. Nor does the Bible translator work with some disembodied "message" or "meaning." He is struggling to establish correspondences between expressions of the different languages involved. He can only operate with these expressions and not with wordless ideas that he might imagine lie behind them. Translators must not undervalue the complex relationship between form and meaning.[9]

The whole dynamic equivalent project is based on an impossibility and a misconception about the relationship between words and meaning.

Someone has accurately said that "the word may be regarded as the body of the thought," adding that "if the words are taken from us, the exact meaning is of itself lost."[10] It is easy to illustrate the dependence of meaning on words by comparing English translations of identical Bible passages. Psalm 1:3 ends with a statement of the complete prosperity of the godly person. Presumably all translators begin in agreement on the gist or general meaning of the statement. But once they commit themselves to the words of a translation, it turns out that the meaning is not independent of the words that express it but instead is determined by those words.

Here is how a range of translations express the agreed-upon meaning:

- "Whatsoever he doeth shall prosper" (KJV).
- "In all that he does, he prospers" (RSV, ESV; NASB similar).
- "In all that they do, they prosper" (NRSV; NLT nearly identical).

- "Whatever he does prospers" (NIV).
- "They succeed in everything they do" (GNB).

Do these translations communicate the same meaning? No. To project prosperity into the future with the formula "shall prosper" is not the same as to assert the present reality that the godly person "prospers." To locate the prosperity in the person by saying that in all that the godly person does "*he* prospers" is different from saying that "whatever he *does*" or "they do" prospers. To paint a portrait of the godly person (singular) communicates a different meaning from the communal or group implication of the plural "they."

What we see in microcosm here is a universal principle: When the words differ, the meaning differs. To claim that we can translate ideas *instead of words* is an impossibility. In the Eugene Nida interview published in *Christianity Today*, Nida was asked, "What units of written texts carry the most meaning?" He replied, "The phrase." To which I ask, "Of what do phrases consist?" The answer, obviously, is "words." To bypass words in favor of thought is a classic case of bypassing what is *primary and precedent* and instead choosing what is *secondary and subsequent*.

3

TEN REASONS WE CAN TRUST ESSENTIALLY LITERAL BIBLE TRANSLATIONS

WHAT IS THE ANTIDOTE to what I have outlined above concerning the negative effects of dynamic equivalent Bible translations? The antidote is an essentially literal translation, and as I move toward saying something about why and how you can trust an essentially literal translation, I want to assert two preliminary points.

The first is this: In a majority of cases where dynamic equivalent translators believe that they need to clarify or explain or change the original, the original authors *could have said it that way* and chose not to. They had the linguistic resources to say it the way modern translators have rendered it. If the biblical authors and the Divine Author who inspired them had thought that the Hebrew epithet translated literally as "Lord of hosts" was beyond the grasp of their audience, they could have used a different Hebrew epithet to express "the Lord almighty." They had the linguistic resources to state it that way. Paul could have urged believers to *live* worthy of the Gospel rather than *walk* worthy of the Gospel (see Eph. 4:1; Col. 1:10; 1 Thess. 2:12). To claim (as dynamic equivalent translators often do) that Paul *intended* to say that we are to *live* worthy of the Gospel is to abuse the normal way in which we use the concept of intention. What an author intended to say is what he *did* say.

Related to this, secondly, is that in the majority of instances in which dynamic equivalent translators claim that they are objecting to literal translations, their actual opponent is not literal translations but the original text of the Bible. When Eugene Nida says that when English translations preserve Mark's stylistic trait of using the connectives *kai* ("and") or *euthys* ("immediately") the effect is "childish,"[11] his complaint is not, as he implies, with literal translations but instead with Mark himself and with the inspired words of the Divine Author as expressed in the original.

Why and how can you trust an essentially literal English translation of the Bible? For the following ten reasons:

1. Transparency to the Original

Except where a completely literal translation would have been unintelligible to an English reader, an essentially literal translation is transparent to the original text.

An essentially literal translation resists inserting an intermediary interpretive process between the reader and the original text. When on rare occasions an essentially literal translation contains something other than an expression of the actual words used by a biblical author, it normally contains as well an accompanying note that gives the literal rendering.[12]

I myself can conceive of no other reason for translation than that it brings a reader as close to the original text as the process of translation allows. Why else would I read a translation of a text? Please note that this is a different kind of transparency than dynamic equivalent translators claim—namely, a translation that is immediately transparent to the contemporary English reader.

It is important to remember that the Bible is not a simple book and that nowhere does it imply that it is immediately and easily understandable to every reader or listener. Contrary to the prefaces of some contemporary translations that are fearful of retaining any statement whose meaning is not immediately clear, Jesus' own theory of communication rested on what I call delayed-action insight. We know from Jesus' explanation of why he spoke in parables that he did *not* intend that everyone would immediately understand his sayings and parables (Mark 4:10-23). If we then look at the actual sayings and parables that Jesus uttered, it is obvious that they do *not* carry all of their meaning on the surface. They require pondering and interpretation and mulling over. They are close relatives of the riddle. They yield their meanings only to those who, metaphorically speaking, "have ears to hear," that is, who take the time to ponder them.

2. KEEPING TO THE ESSENTIAL TASK OF TRANSLATION

You can trust an essentially literal translation to keep to the essential task of translation—namely, translation.

This is a way of saying that an essentially literal translation is not the product of a translation committee's going beyond translation to the additional tasks of an editor and exegete, either substituting material in the place of what the original says or adding interpretive commentary to the biblical text.

3. PRESERVING THE FULL INTERPRETIVE POTENTIAL OF THE ORIGINAL

You can trust an essentially literal translation to preserve the full interpretive potential of the original text.

An essentially literal translation resists the following common forms of reductionism that afflict dynamic equivalent translations.[13]

- simplifying the original text to a lowest common denominator of contemporary readers;
- choosing just one of the potential meanings of a passage and putting only that in front of the reader;

- making preemptive interpretive strikes so as to prevent the reader from making interpretive decisions for himself or herself;
- eliminating technical or difficult theological vocabulary and substituting non-technical vocabulary;
- interpreting figurative language right in the translation;
- assuming that modern readers are inferior to both the original audience of the Bible and to readers of the English Bible through the centuries;
- reducing the level of vocabulary;
- diminishing the literary beauty and exaltation of the Bible;
- paring down the affective power of the Bible;
- reducing the stylistic variety of the original text to a monotone arrived at by slanting the translation toward a target audience with allegedly low linguistic and cognitive abilities.

Stated positively, you can trust an essentially literal translation to do the following things as a way of preserving the full richness and exegetical potential of the Bible: An essentially literal translation seeks to preserve . . .

- language as beautiful and sophisticated as the original itself possesses;
- as many levels of meaning as the original contains;
- poetry in its original, literal expression;
- the stylistic range of the original;
- theological terminology as complex as the original contains.

The goal of an essentially literal translation is fullness. The effect of dynamic equivalent translations has been diminishment—diminishment in the form of reduced expectations of Bible readers, reduced respect for biblical authors (I think here partly of the "what Paul was *trying* to say" condescension), impoverishment of language, emaciated theology, a one-dimensional Bible in regard to legitimate multiple meanings, and lowered literary standards.

4. NOT MIXING COMMENTARY WITH TRANSLATION

You can trust an essentially literal translation not to mislead you by mixing commentary and translation.

We normally operate on the premise that the book that a publisher or translator puts into our hands is what the original author actually wrote. Within the necessary changes that all translation requires, an essentially literal translation does not betray that trust. It keeps to an absolute minimum the intermingling of interpretive commentary with translation. An essentially literal translation operates on the premise that a translator is a steward of what someone else has written, not an editor and exegete who needs to explain or correct what someone else has written.

5. PRESERVING THEOLOGICAL PRECISION

You can trust an essentially literal translation to preserve theological precision.

We cannot build an adequate theology without an adequate theological vocabulary. A theological concept of justification can be built on the statement (Romans 3:24) that "we are justified by his grace as a gift" (ESV), but not on such dynamic equivalent paraphrases as "we are put right with [God]" (GNB) or "God in his gracious kindness declares us not guilty" (NLT) or "God treats us much better than we deserve" (CEV).

6. Not Needing to Correct the Translation in Preaching

You can trust an essentially literal translation to preserve an expository preacher from needing to correct the translation from which he is preaching.

Professor Jack Collins of Covenant Seminary began his ministerial career as a preacher. He recalls his increasing uneasiness about the discrepancy between what his parishioners' translations said and what he knew the original said. The more he corrected their translations, the more he suspected that his parishioners would come to distrust the reliability of the Bible.

7. Preserving What the Biblical Writers Actually Wrote

You can trust an essentially literal translation not to resolve all interpretive difficulties in the direction of what a given translation committee decides to parcel out to its readers.

Instead you can expect a literal translation to pass on interpretive difficulties to the reader. Is this a virtue? Indeed it is. The goal is to know what the original authors said. If they passed difficulties on to *their* readers, translators need to do the same.

8. Preserving the Literary Qualities of the Bible

If your essentially literal translation is the RSV, the ESV, or the NKJV—in other words, if your essentially literal translation rides the literary coattails of the matchless KJV—you can trust it to preserve the literary qualities of the Bible that the KJV gave to the English-speaking world for nearly four centuries.

The Bible in its original is a very literary book, and I have based half of a scholarly career on that premise. We need to understand that if we believe that the Holy Spirit inspired the authors of the Bible, it was ultimately the Holy Spirit who gave us a literary Bible replete with poetry, for example. It was the Holy Spirit who gave us figurative language, and an essentially literal translation preserves that figurative language.

9. PRESERVING THE DIGNITY AND BEAUTY OF THE BIBLE

You can trust some essentially literal translations to preserve the exaltation, dignity, and beauty of the Bible.

You can expect to read, "Behold, I stand at the door and knock" (Rev. 3:20, KJV, NASB, ESV), not such things as this: "Here I am! I stand at the door and knock" (NIV, TNIV), or, "Here I stand knocking at the door" (REB), or, "Listen! I am standing and knocking at your door" (CEV). In an essentially literal translation you will find the awe-inspiring lead-in, "Truly, truly, I say to you" (ESV), not a translation that has scaled the voltage down to "I tell you the truth" (NIV) or "I tell you for certain" (CEV) or "I assure you" (NLT). An essentially literal translation will fire your imagination and wonder with its evocative picture of "ivory palaces" (Ps. 45:8, KJV, NASB, ESV), not such mundane versions as "palaces adorned with ivory" (NIV) or "palaces panelled with ivory" (REB) or "palaces decorated with ivory" (GNB, NLT).

10. CONSISTENCY WITH THE DOCTRINE OF INSPIRATION

You can trust an essentially literal translation to be most consistent with the doctrine of plenary or verbal inspiration.

Such a translation believes that the very words of the Bible are inspired and therefore inviolable—that the revelation of God resides in the words themselves, not merely in thoughts or ideas.

Throughout the Bible, Scripture is referred to as the word of God, not the thought(s) of God. Jesus himself said that "*the words* that I have spoken to you are spirit and life" (John 6:63, ESV; italics added), leading Luther to note that "Christ did not say of His thoughts, but of His words, that they are spirit and life."[14]

CONCLUSION

English Bible translation stands at a watershed moment. For half a century, dynamic equivalence has been the guiding translation philosophy behind most new translations. Each successive wave of these translations has tended to be increasingly bold in departing from the words of the original text. Stated another way, we can trace an arc of increasingly aggressive changing, adding to, and subtracting from the words that the biblical authors wrote. The issues that are at stake in the current debate about Bible translation are immense.

NOTES

1. Alister McGrath, *In the Beginning: The Story of the King James Bible and How It Changed a Nation, a Language, and a Culture* (New York: Doubleday, 2001), 250.

2. For examples of how the prefaces of essentially literal translations claim fidelity to the words of the original, see Leland Ryken, *The Word of God in English: Criteria for Excellence in Bible Translation* (Wheaton, IL: Crossway Books, 2002), 134.

3. "Meaning-full Translations," *Christianity Today*, October 7, 2002: 46-49.

4. The main exceptions to this are the *New American Standard Bible* (NASB, 1963; and updated NASB, 1995), the New King James Version (NKJV, 1982), the English Standard Version (ESV, 2001), and the Holman Christian Standard Version (HCSB New Testament, 2000; Old Testament 2004).

5. Raymond C. Van Leeuwen, "We Really Do Need Another Bible Translation," *Christianity Today*, October 22, 2001: 29.

6. Jan de Waard and Eugene A. Nida, *From One Language to Another: Functional Equivalence in Bible Translating* (Nashville: Thomas Nelson, 1986), 39.

7. Incidentally, three times during the sermon this preacher invoked the familiar formula, "Now what the original really says is . . ." as he needed to correct his dynamic equivalent translation, whereas if he had been using a literal translation he would not have needed to invoke this formula at all.

8. Van Leeuwen, "We Really Do Need Another Bible Translation," 30.

9. Anthony Howard Nichols, "Translating the Bible: A Critical Analysis of E. A. Nida's Theory of Dynamic Equivalence and Its Impact Upon Recent Bible Translations," dissertation, University of Sheffield, 1996, 295.

10. Erich Sauer, *From Eternity to Eternity*, trans. G. H. Land (London: Paternoster, 1954), 103.

11. Eugene A. Nida and Charles R. Taber, *The Theory and Practice of Translation* (Leiden: E. J. Brill, 1969), 13.

12. Concerning the translation of idioms, biblical scholar Wayne Grudem notes: "Everyone agrees that difficult idioms need to be handled as exceptions. But that is not the question. The question is: Is the meaning of every word in Greek or Hebrew represented in the English translation, or just left out? In dynamic equivalent translations, much meaning is left out. In essentially literal translations, sometimes the meaning of a Greek word is just represented by a question mark or a comma in English, but the meaning is still represented. Sometimes one word is translated by two or three English words, sometimes two or three Greek words are translated by one English word, but in every case the meaning of every word in the original is represented by the translation. We need to ask, 'How does this translation represent the force of this or that Greek word in the original?' and we need to provide an answer for that. Dynamic equivalent translations, however, make the exceptions (the idioms, which are always hard to translate) into a general policy. They fail to translate the words where it makes perfectly good sense to translate the words. That is our objection."

13. For more on each one, see *The Word of God in English* (Wheaton, IL: Crossway Books, 2002).

14. Martin Luther, as quoted in René Paché, *The Inspiration and Authority of Scripture*, trans. Helen I. Needham (Chicago: Moody Press, 1969), 75.

APPENDIX: BIBLE TRANSLATIONS CHART

This is a chart of selected translations and the philosophies behind them; it is not meant to be precise. The format below shows two things: (1) There is a continuum extending from the NASB down to The Street Bible, but (2) there are three distinct translation philosophies, and there is a marked difference between an "essentially literal" translation, a "dynamic equivalent" translation, and a paraphrase. The upper-left represents more literal translation, and the bottom-right represents less literal translation.

Essentially Literal
NASB   ESV   KJV/NKJV   RSV/NRSV

Dynamic Equivalent
NIV   TNIV   NLT   CEV   GNB

Paraphrase
NTME   TLB   TM   TSB

Key of Abbreviations:
NASB—New American Standard Bible
ESV—English Standard Standard
NKJV—New King James Version
KJV—King James Version
RSV—Revised Standard Version
NRSV—New Revised Standard Version
NIV—New International Version
TNIV—Today's New International Version
NLT—New Living Translation
CEV—Contemporary English Version
GNB—Good News Bible
NTME—The NT in Modern English (Phillips)
TLB—The Living Bible
TM—The Message
TSB—The Street Bible